Matinicus Rock Lighthouse,
Maine

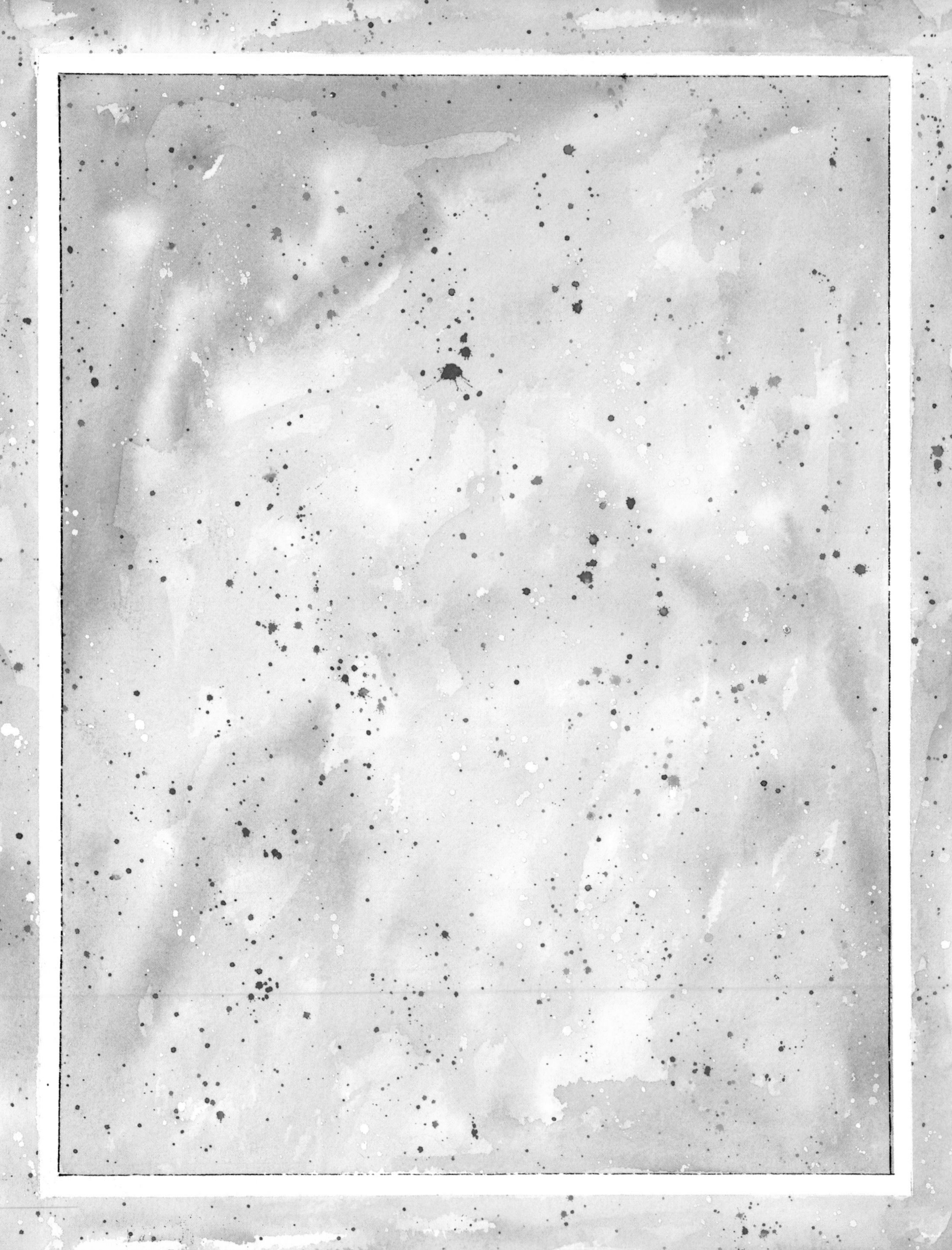

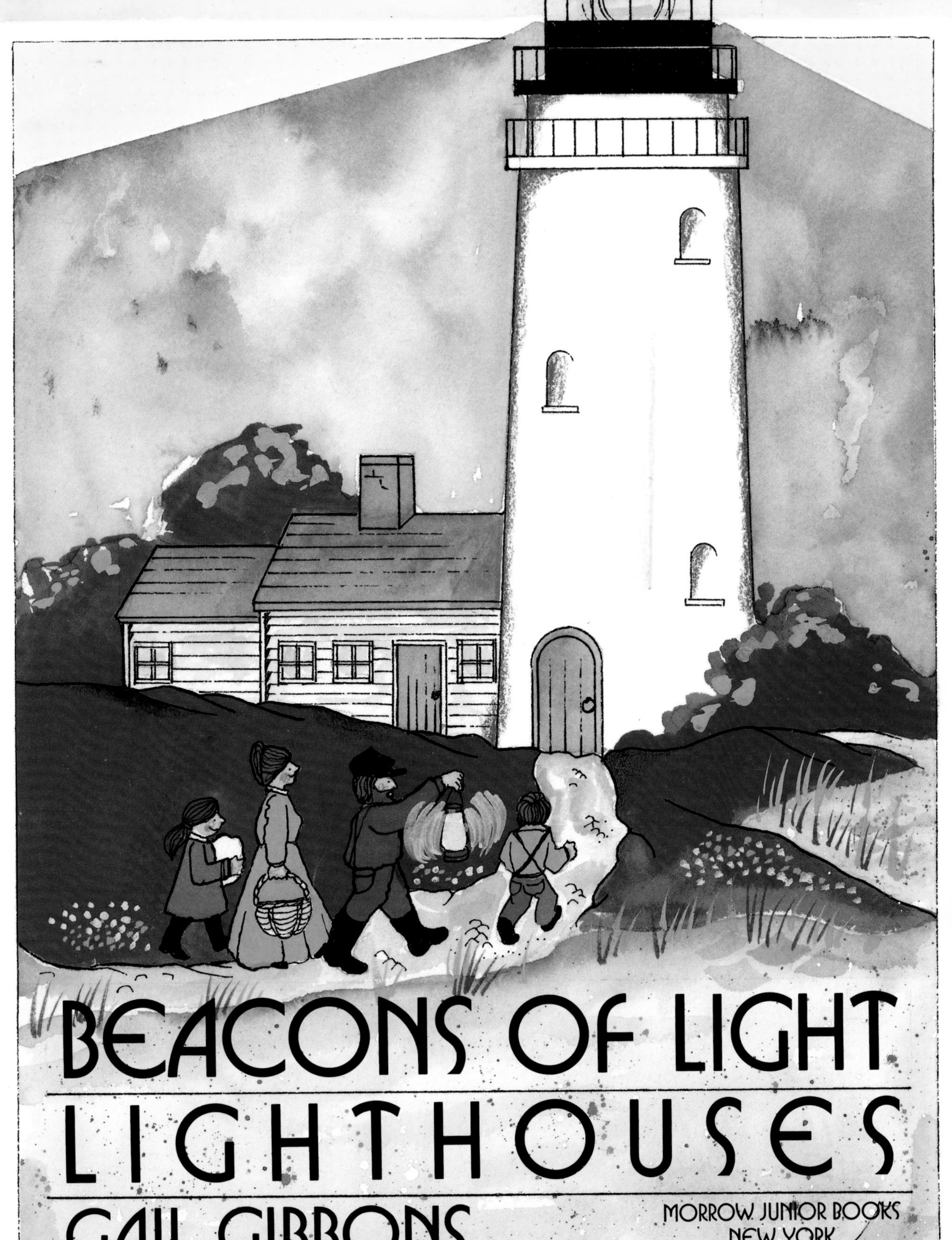
BEACONS OF LIGHT
LIGHTHOUSES
GAIL GIBBONS
MORROW JUNIOR BOOKS
NEW YORK

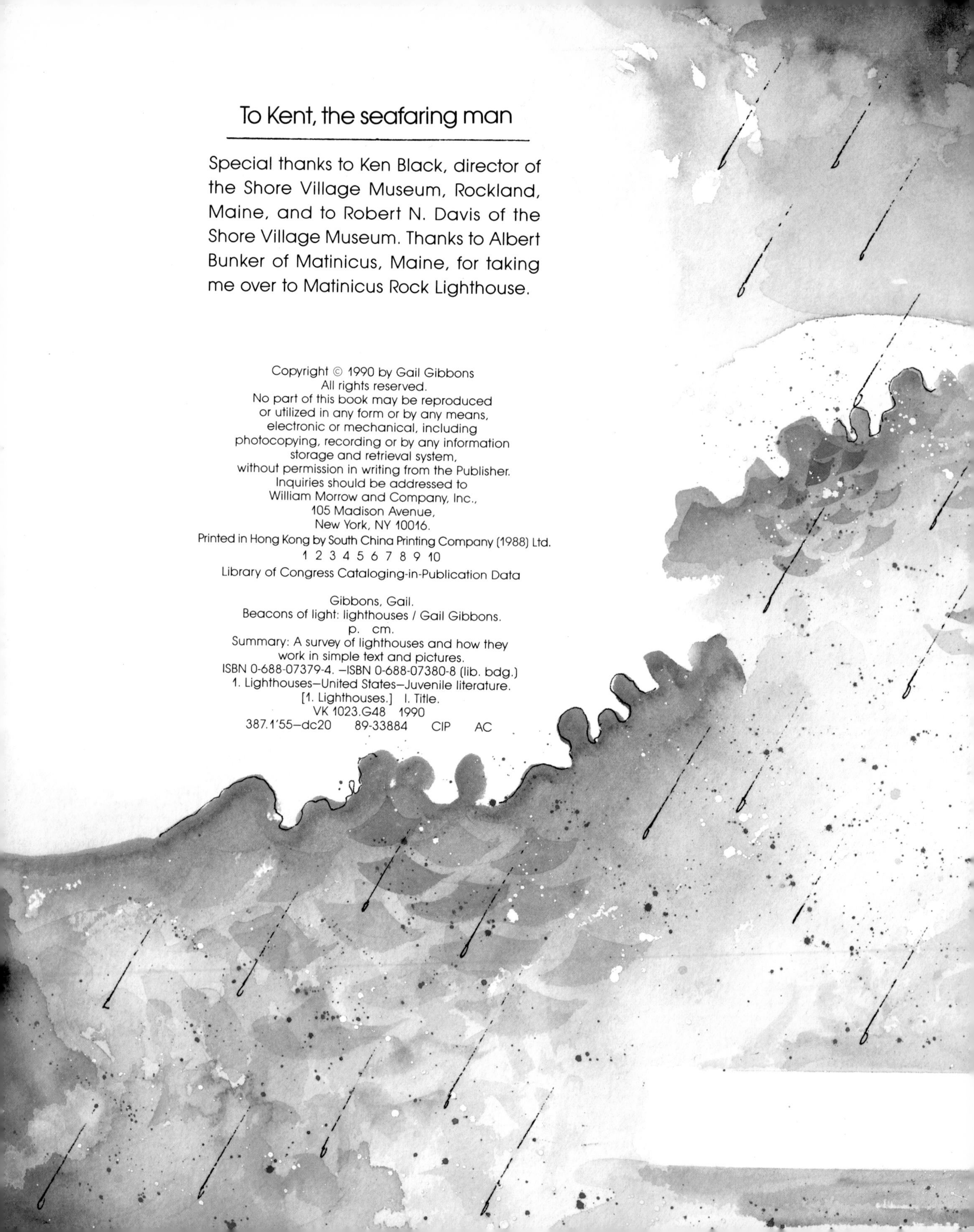

To Kent, the seafaring man

Special thanks to Ken Black, director of the Shore Village Museum, Rockland, Maine, and to Robert N. Davis of the Shore Village Museum. Thanks to Albert Bunker of Matinicus, Maine, for taking me over to Matinicus Rock Lighthouse.

Inquiries should be addressed to
William Morrow and Company, Inc.,
105 Madison Avenue,
New York, NY 10016.
Printed in Hong Kong by South China Printing Company (1988) Ltd.
1 2 3 4 5 6 7 8 9 10
Library of Congress Cataloging-in-Publication Data

Gibbons, Gail.
Beacons of light: lighthouses / Gail Gibbons.
p. cm.
Summary: A survey of lighthouses and how they
work in simple text and pictures.
ISBN 0-688-07379-4. –ISBN 0-688-07380-8 (lib. bdg.)
1. Lighthouses–United States–Juvenile literature.
[1. Lighthouses.] I. Title.
VK 1023.G48 1990
387.1'55–dc20 89-33884 CIP AC

Waves thrash and winds swirl, tossing a ship about in the darkness.

Then, in the distance, a light appears. It flashes three times, disappears, then flashes again.

On board, the ship's crew recognizes that this is a lighthouse signal. It is telling them to veer away from something hidden beneath the water. The captain locates a rocky ledge on his chart and uses the light signal to plot their position.

Oceans and lakes have always been dangerous for sailors. Storms and howling winds can carry a ship up on a sandbar or smash it to bits against a rocky coast.

Lighthouses help guide ships and boats safely from one place to another. They warn of dangerous rocks and ledges, hidden points of land, sandbars, and narrow entrances to harbors.

The first guiding lights were huge bonfires that burned brightly from the tops of hills. In some places, sailors watched for landmarks, such as volcanoes, glowing in the night.

For thousands of years, light signals didn't change very much. When lighthouses were built, they were often stone towers with fires burning at the top.

The first lighthouse in North America was the Boston Light, built in 1716. From Little Brewster Island, it guided sailing vessels in and out of Boston harbor.

Over the next hundred years, many more lighthouses were built. Most were round and narrowed off at the top to resist wind and stormy seas. The light was placed high to be seen at a distance.

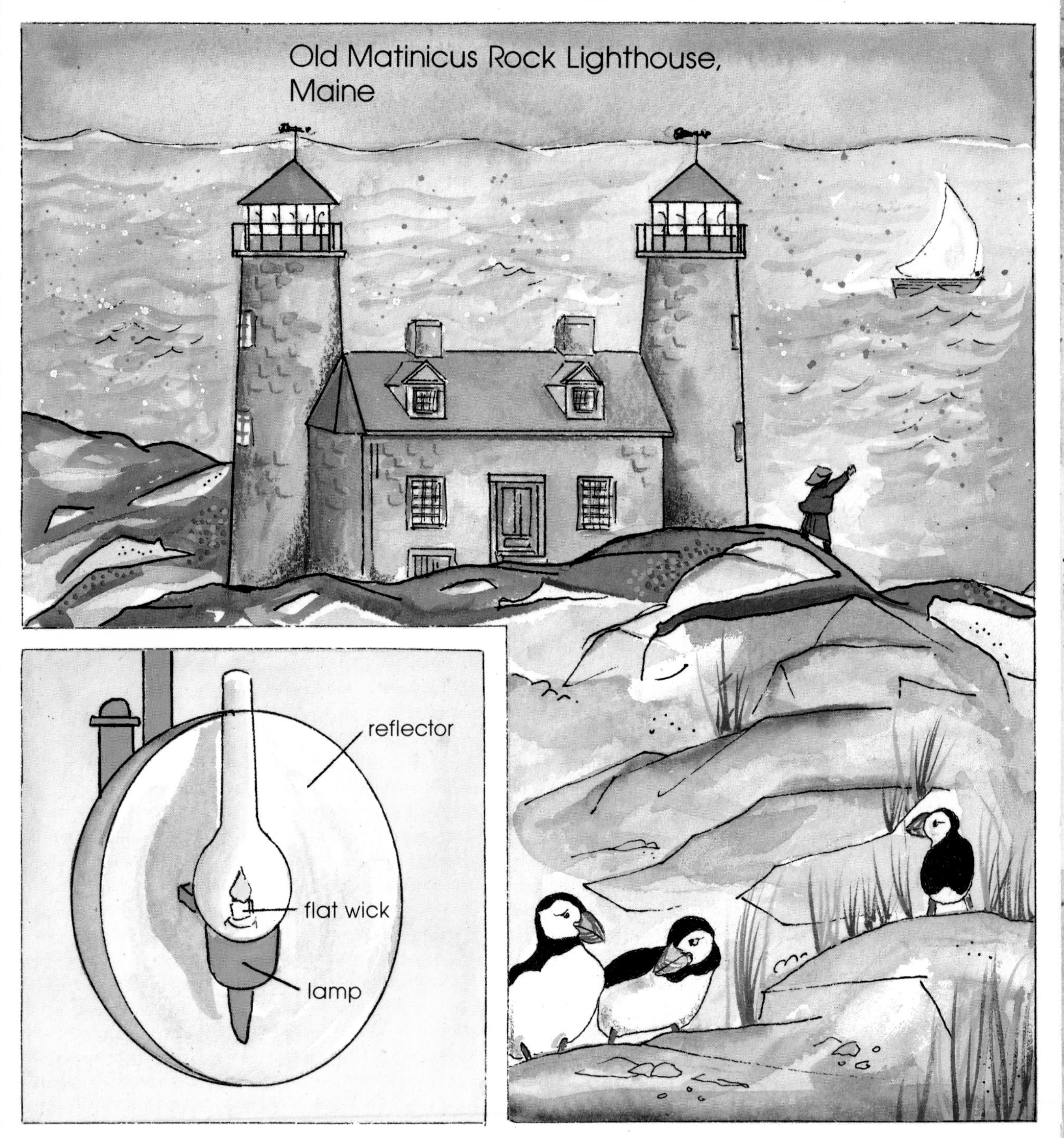

These early lighthouses used wick lamps as a source of light, burning whale oil or fish oil for fuel. The lighthouse keepers learned to increase the lamps' brightness by placing reflectors behind them.

Thatcher's Island Lighthouse, Massachusetts

In 1782, a Swiss scientist, Aimé Argand, developed a brighter lamp. It had a circular wick. When whale oil became scarce, colza (a form of vegetable oil), lard (from animal fat), and, later, kerosene were used.

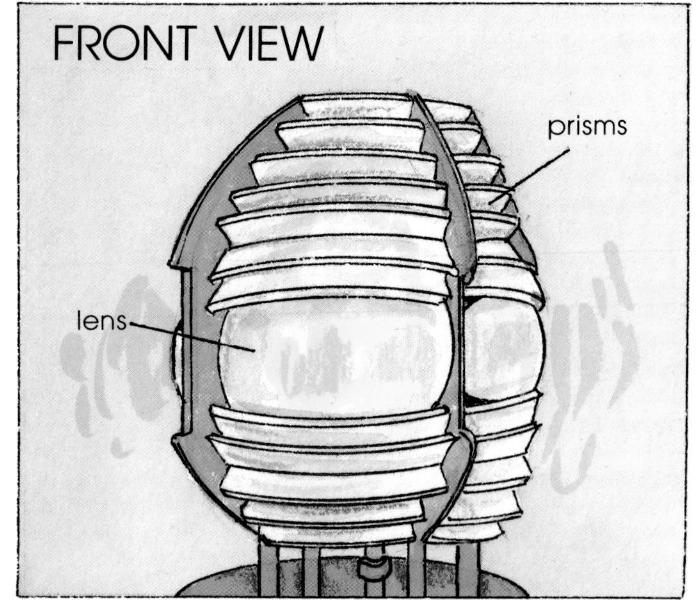

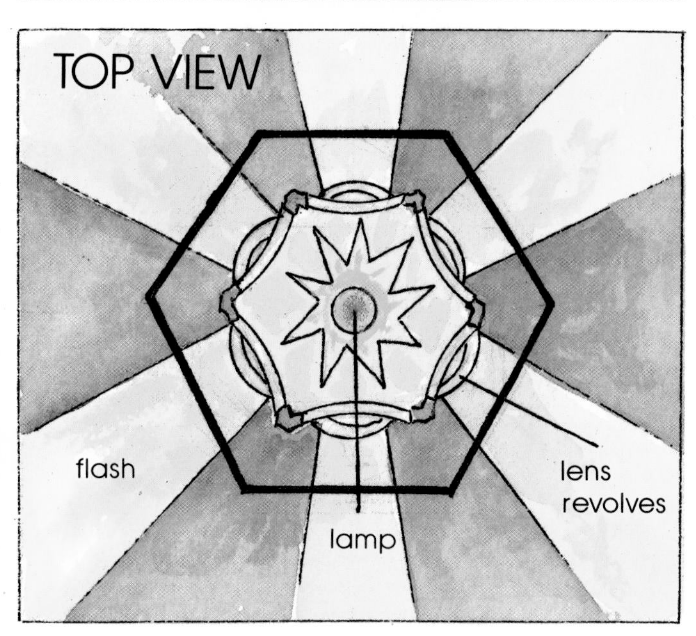

At that time, signals from lighthouses were visible only a few miles, even on a clear night. Then, in 1822, the first modern lighthouse lens was invented by a Frenchman named Augustin Fresnel, who found a way to increase the light by using prisms. The prisms of the lens bent the light beam and concentrated it, making the light visible for many miles.

In 1841, the Fresnel lens was installed for the first time in a lighthouse in the United States. Its beam could be seen twenty miles away at night.

The top of a lighthouse is like a giant lantern. Usually, a winding staircase goes to the top. Years ago, the lighthouse keeper made many trips up and down the stairs, doing chores. The burned lamp wick had to be *trimmed*—or adjusted and cut off—to keep the lamp from smoking. Lighthouse keepers were sometimes called *wick trimmers* or *wickies.*

Lighthouse keepers and their families were kept busy cleaning and polishing the lenses, shining all the brass in the lighthouse, and cleaning soot off the tower windows.

The keeper's house stood near or was attached to the base of the lighthouse. Sometimes, the keeper lived right inside the lighthouse. Often, there were a number of other structures around the lighthouse, called *outbuildings*.

Everything in and around the lighthouse was kept tidy. All of these buildings had to be maintained and frequently painted. It was hard work.

Some lighthouses were built on remote islands or isolated spits of land. Many lighthouse keepers led lonely lives, without company for weeks at a time.

During storms, their work could be very dangerous. Great waves would crash against the coast and strong winds would blow. Sometimes there were disasters—shipwrecks! The lighthouse keeper would have to help rescue and shelter poor souls who had been cast adrift in the sea.

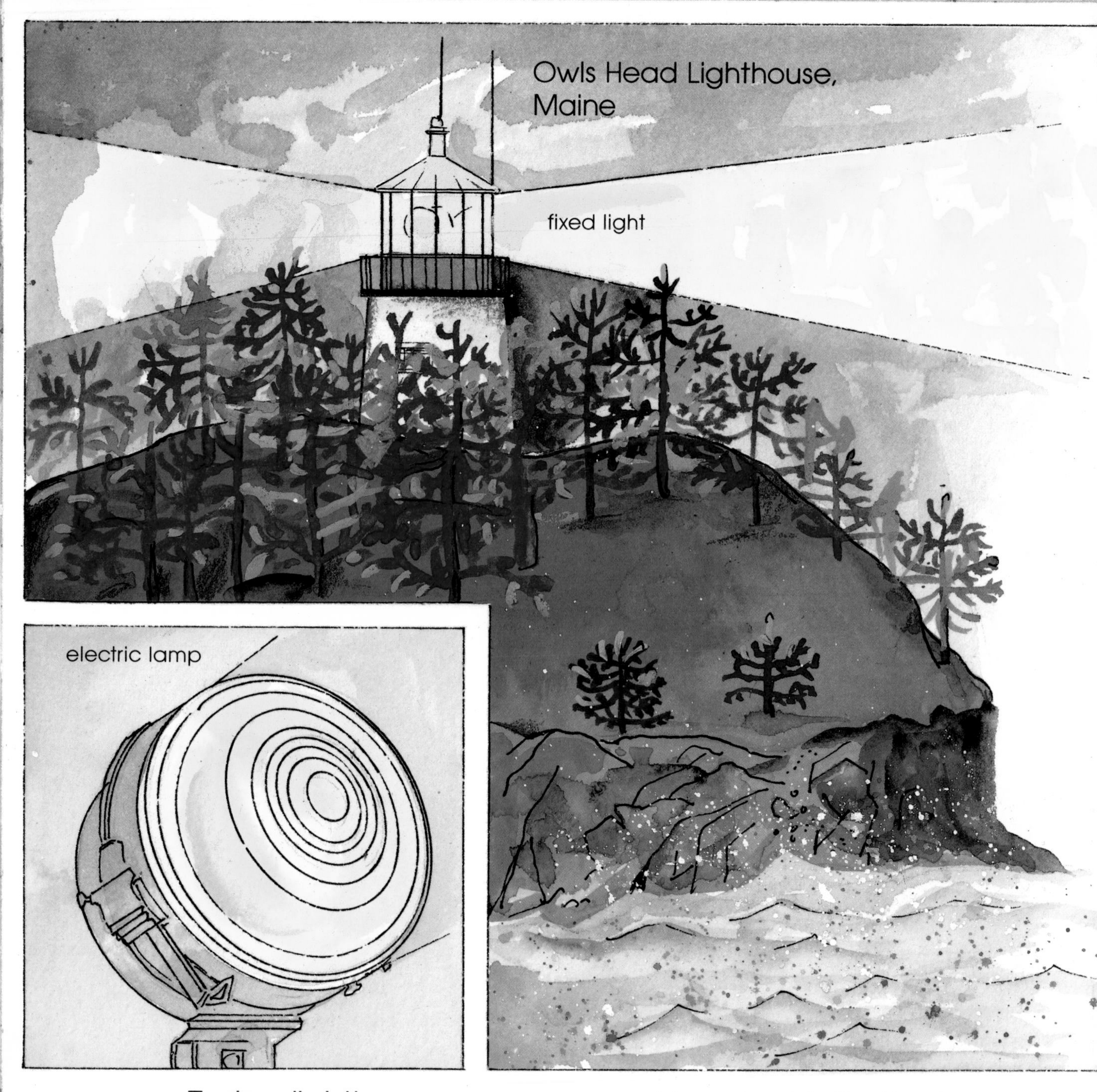

Today, lighthouses are powered by electricity. Each lighthouse has its own identifying signal, called its *characteristic.* There are several kinds of lighthouse signals. A light that shines all the time is called a *fixed light.*

A *flashing light* has periods of darkness longer than its periods of light.

A *group flashing light* gives off two or more flashes at regular intervals. All lighthouse lights are white, red, green, or a combination of these three colors.

After sighting and timing the flashes of a lighthouse, a ship's captain refers to a *light list*. From this list, the captain can determine what lighthouse is in view and can then figure the ship's location from looking at the charts.

During daylight hours, a particular lighthouse can be identified by its distinctive shape or painted pattern.

When heavy fog settles in, lighthouses are difficult to see. For a time, cannons were used to warn ships and boats away from danger in a fog. Shots were fired each hour. Later, lighthouse keepers rang bells, and sometimes guns, sirens, or whistles were used as danger signals.

Today, at many lighthouse sites, foghorns give off warnings. Each foghorn has its own special sound and number of blasts.

The *diaphone,* one of the best foghorns, uses compressed air to give off two tones, a high-pitched screech and a low grunt. The high sound can be heard for seven miles. The low tone travels farther. Lighthouses also use radio beacons to send warning signals.

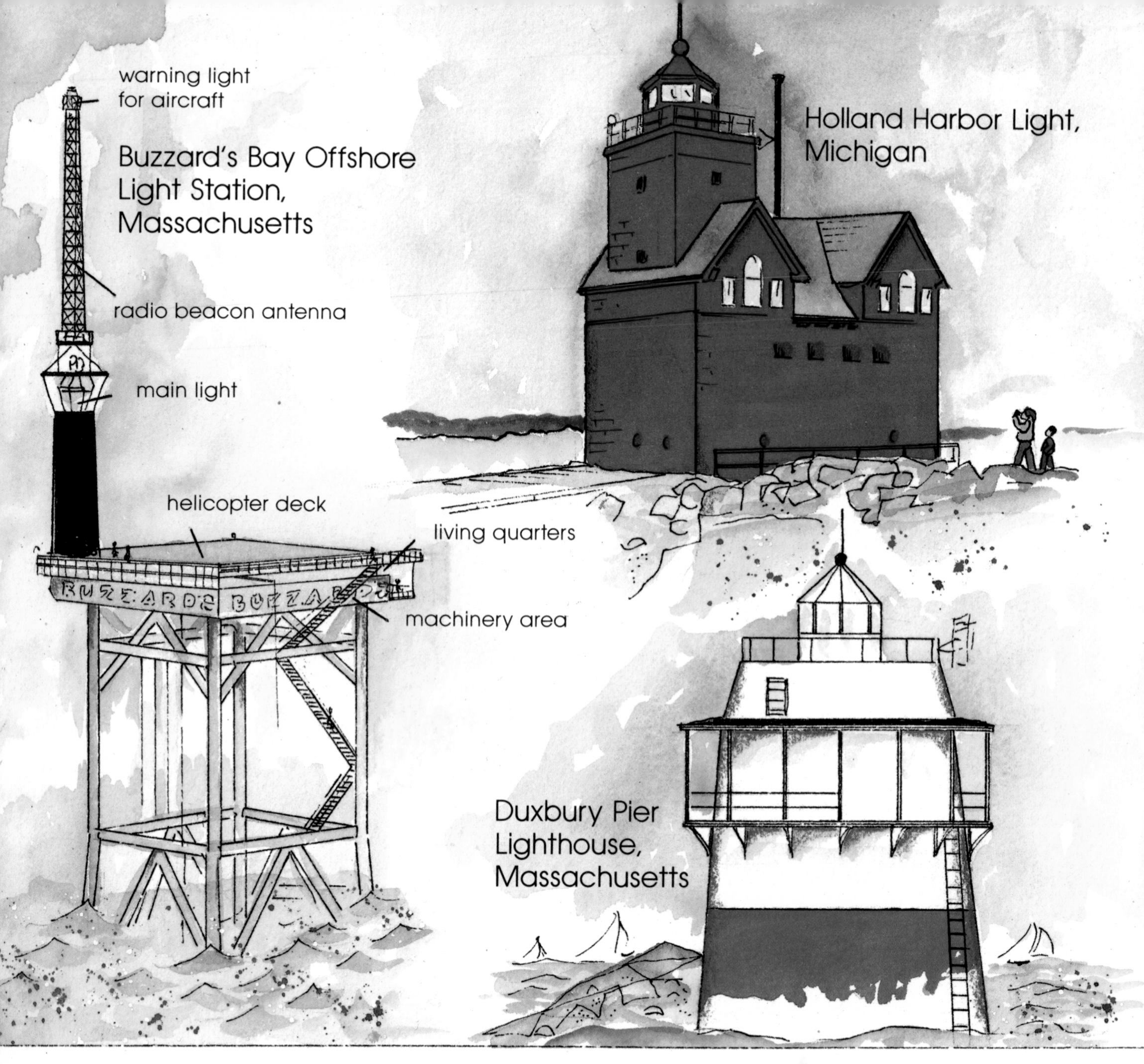

Lighthouses come in many different sizes and shapes. Each was built to fit its own individual requirements and location. Some of the newer lighthouses stand on stilts and hardly look like lighthouses at all.

Now, there are very few lighthouse keepers needed. Some lights stay on all the time. Others go on and off automatically. They are maintained by the Coast Guard. Although they have changed over the years, lighthouses are still beacons of light to guide and warn of danger and to remind us of the past.

FLASH...FLASH...FLASH

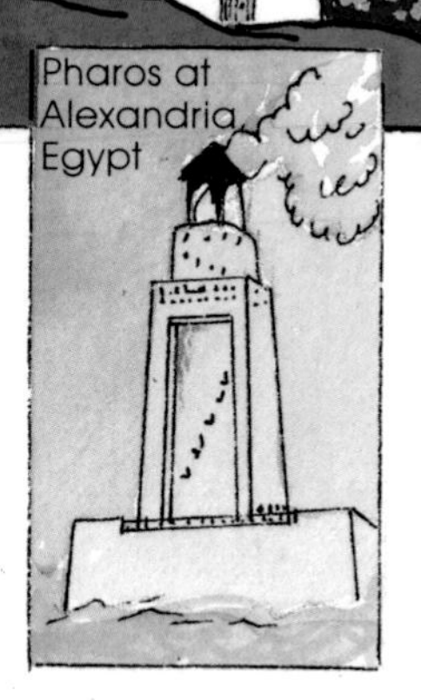

The first lighthouses were towers, built about 2,000 years ago: the Pharos at Alexandria, in Egypt, and the Colossus at Rhodes, an island off Greece.

In the United States, there are about 500 operating lighthouses.

For many years, lightships were used as floating lighthouses. None of these are in use today.

Many years ago, a woman named Ida Lewis was the keeper of the Lime Rock Lighthouse in Rhode Island. During her lifetime, she saved the lives of more than a dozen people while on duty.

At Owls Head Light in Maine, a famous dog, Spot, used to ring the bell when fog settled in.

In the last century, a girl named Abbie Burgess kept the lights burning during a storm at Matinicus Rock Lighthouse off the coast of Maine. The storm blew up while her father was away from the island getting supplies. She tended the lights for four weeks all by herself.

The first electrified lighthouse was the Statue of Liberty, erected in 1886.

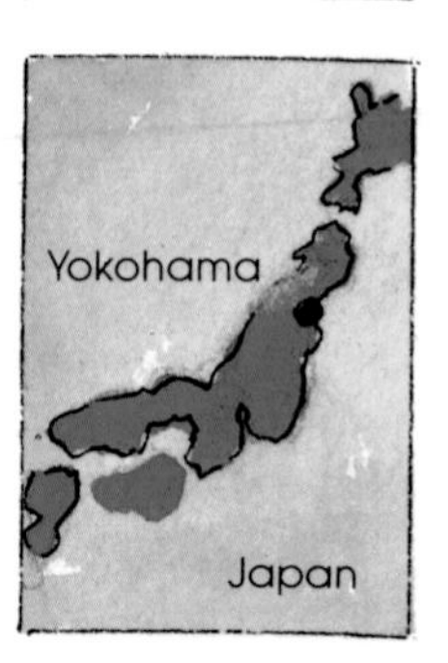

The tallest lighthouse is a 348-foot-high tower in Yokohama, Japan.

CCDC 7/09
LPS 8/09